A Note to Parents and Caregivers:

Read-it! Joke Books are for children who are moving ahead on the amazing road to reading. These fun books support the acquisition and extension of reading skills as well as a love of books.

Published by the same company that produces *Read-it!* Readers, these books introduce the question/answer and dialogue patterns that help children expand their thinking about language structure and book formats.

When sharing joke books with a child, read in short stretches. Pause often to talk about the meaning of the jokes. The question/answer and dialogue formats work well for this purpose and provide an opportunity to talk about the language and meaning of the jokes. Have the child turn the pages and point to the pictures and familiar words. When you read the jokes, have fun creating the voices of characters or emphasizing some important words. Be sure to reread favorite jokes.

There is no right or wrong way to share books with children. Find time to read with your child, and pass on the legacy of literacy.

Adria F. Klein, Ph.D.
Professor Emeritus
California State University
San Bernardino, California

Editor: Jill Kalz
Designer: Joe Anderson
Page Production: Melissa Kes
Creative Director: Keith Griffin
Editorial Director: Carol Jones
The illustrations in this book were created digitally.

Picture Window Books
5115 Excelsior Boulevard
Suite 232
Minneapolis, MN 55416
877-845-8392
www.picturewindowbooks.com

Printed in the United States of America.

Library of Congress Cataloging-in-Publication Data
Donahue, Jill L.
What's in a name? : a book of name jokes / by Jill L. Donahue ; illustrated by
Zachary Trover.
p. cm. – (Read-it! joke books–supercharged!)
Includes bibliographical references.
ISBN-13: 978-1-4048-2364-8 (hardcover)
ISBN-10: 1-4048-2364-6 (hardcover)
1. Names, Personal–Juvenile humor. 2. Riddles, Juvenile. I. Trover, Zachary. II. Title.
III. Title: What is in a name? IV. Series.
PN6231.N24D66 2006
818'.602–dc22   2006003570

in a
NAME?

A Book of Name Jokes

by Jill L. Donahue
illustrated by Zachary Trover

Special thanks to our advisers for their expertise:

Adria F. Klein, Ph.D.
Professor Emeritus, California State University
San Bernardino, California

Susan Kesselring, M.A.
Literacy Educator
Rosemount–Apple Valley–Eagan (Minnesota) School District

PICTURE WINDOW BOOKS
Minneapolis, Minnesota

What do you call a woman who loves to gamble?

Betty.

What do you call a girl with a golden tan?

Amber.

What do you call a man who loves to work on old cars?

Rusty.

What do you call a man who is an underwater spy?
James Pond.

What do you call a boy who lives on a dirt road?
Dusty.

What do you call a boy who sits on top of a present?

Bo.

What do you call a man who builds railroad tracks?

Spike.

What do you call a woman who studies weather and the wind?

Gail.

What do you call a man who raises bees?
Buzz.

What do you call a girl who wakes up before the sun rises?
Dawn.

What do you call a girl who lives on a narrow street in the middle of the block?
Ally.

What do you call a boy who gives away a lot of money?
Grant.

8

What do you call a woman who is good at fixing flat tires?

Erin.

What do you call a girl who likes to touch all of the animals at the zoo?

Pat.

What do you call a man who always cuts himself shaving?

Nick.

What do you call a girl who collects coins?

Penny.

What do you call a boy who wants to be the head of a college someday?

Dean.

What do you call a kid who lives on the highway?

Lane.

What do you call a woman who is always happy and cheerful?

Mary.

What do you call a boy who is good at mending clothes?

Taylor.

What do you call a girl who is very beautiful and sparkly?

Crystal.

What do you call a boy who likes to make his bed every day?

Tucker.

12

What do you call a man who has a lot of money?

Rich.

What do you call a boy who lies in the sun all day?

Tanner.

What do you call a girl who hangs on the mantle at Christmastime?

Holly.

What do you call a boy who is very tall?
  Miles.

What do you call a man who gives a lot of support to people?
  Cain.

What do you call a man who can do almost anything he wants to?
Abel.

What do you call a girl who is most active after dinner?
Eve.

What do you call a boy who has a very loud voice?
Mike.

What do you call a woman who gives her stuff to other people?

Sharon.

What do you call a boy who loves to eat cheese dip?

Chip.

What do you call a boy who lives in a mine?

Cole.

What do you call a boy who likes to jump rope?
  Skip.

What do you call a girl who loves cats?
  Kitty.

What do you call a boy who writes on the wall?
Mark.

What do you call a girl with very pink cheeks?
Rosie.

What do you call a boy who loves to throw things?
Chuck.

18

What do you call a boy who races go-carts?
Carter.

What do you call a girl who has words on her front and on her back?
Paige.

What do you call a boy who
lives in a tree?
Leif.

What do you call a boy who can't
draw very well on his own?
Trace.

What do you call a boy who likes
to make pottery?
Clay.

What do you call a woman who is worth a lot of money?

Jewel.

What do you call a boy who has dishes stacked on top of him?

Trey.

What do you call a man who takes other people's things?

Rob.

What do you call a girl who lives in France?

Paris.

What do you call a man who drives a big car that carries lots of passengers?

Van.

What do you call a boy who runs after people all the time?

Chase.

What do you call a woman who loves rainy weather?

Misty.

Read-it! Joke Books—
Supercharged!

 Chitchat Chuckles: A Book of Funny Talk 1-4048-1160-5

Creepy Crawlers: A Book of Bug Jokes 1-4048-0627-X

Fur, Feathers, and Fun! A Book of Animal Jokes 1-4048-1161-3

Lunchbox Laughs: A Book of Food Jokes 1-4048-0963-5

Mind Knots: A Book of Riddles 1-4048-1162-1

Nutty Names: A Book of Name Jokes 1-4048-1163-X

Roaring with Laughter: A Book of Animal Jokes 1-4048-0628-8

Sit! Stay! Laugh! A Book of Pet Jokes 1-4048-0629-6

Wacky Workers: A Book of Job Jokes 1-4048-1164-8

What's Up, Doc? A Book of Doctor Jokes 1-4048-1165-6

 Artful Antics: A Book of Art, Music, and Theater Jokes
1-4048-2363-8

Family Follies: A Book of Family Jokes 1-4048-2362-X

Laughing Letters and Nutty Numerals: A Book of Jokes About
ABCs and 123s 1-4048-2365-4

Looking for a specific title or level? A complete list
of *Read-it!* Readers is available on our Web site:
www.picturewindowbooks.com